The Day Twin and the Night Twin

By Alan Trussell-Cullen

Illustrated by Francis Phillipps

Dominie Press, Inc.

Publisher: Raymond Yuen
Project Editor: John S. F. Graham
Editor: Bob Rowland
Designer: Greg DiGenti
Illustrator: Francis Phillipps

Published by:

🐪 Dominie Press, Inc.

1949 Kellogg Avenue
Carlsbad, California 92008 USA

www.dominie.com

1-800-232-4570

Paperback ISBN 0-7685-1832-6
Printed in Singapore by PH Productions Pte Ltd
1 2 3 4 5 6 PH 05 04 03

Table of Contents

Chapter One
This Will Never Do!

Long, long ago, when all was very new, the world as we know it was empty, except for two giants. Their names were Dawi and Nawi. And even though they were twins, they could not have been more different.

Dawi liked to be doing things. He could never sit still. He had a giant shovel. He looked at the flat, empty Earth and said, "This will never do!"

So he took his giant shovel and began to dig deep holes. And he threw the dirt from the holes into giant piles. The holes filled with water and became lakes and oceans. The dirt piles grew higher and higher, and became hills and mountains.

Nawi, however, liked to make things. She liked to make little things, delicate things. She had a giant sewing basket with a giant pair of scissors and a needle and pins and a giant ball of invisible thread. She looked at the bare, empty earth and said, "This will never do!"

So she took her giant sewing basket and began to cut out the shapes of leaves and flowers and trees. Then she took her

giant needle and invisible thread and began to stitch them together to make all the things that live and grow on the Earth.

Nawi and Dawi liked to work together. Dawi liked the trees and flowers that his sister had made, so he took his shovel and patted down some of the mountains to make plains and meadows for them. He dug trenches in the plains and meadows to provide more water for them to grow. These became the rivers and streams.

Nawi liked her brother's mountains, lakes, and oceans so much that she made some of her trees and flowers especially for them. For the mountains, she made trees that had strong roots so they would stay upright. For the oceans, she made underwater plants and trees that could grow in salty water. And even in places where there weren't any rivers, she made flowers that didn't need much water in order to grow.

They liked each other's work, but there was one thing they couldn't agree on.

In those days, the sun shone all the time. There was no night, only day. So when Dawi and Nawi felt tired, they would just curl up on the ground and sleep.

The only trouble was, Nawi found it very hard to sleep with the sun shining.

Chapter Two
The Night Blanket

"I can't sleep with all this light. I want it to be dark," Nawi said.

"But Sister," Dawi said, "I like sleeping with the light all around me. I don't like the dark. It frightens me."

Nawi didn't want to upset her brother,

but she didn't want to remain sleepless, either. She tried sleeping with her eyes in the shade of her tall trees, but there was still too much sunlight. She tried sleeping in the dark shadows of the mountains, but there was still too much sunlight.

One day, Nawi decided she could not stand sleeping in the bright sunlight any longer. She took out her giant sewing basket and stitched together a huge black cloth. She called it her "night blanket."

When it was finished, she did not show it to her brother. She knew he was frightened of the darkness and wouldn't like even looking at it.

At first, she tried sleeping with her night blanket over just herself, but she found that it was too warm with the sunlight falling directly on it.

So she sighed and said, "I'm sorry," to her sleeping brother. "But I have to be able to sleep."

She pulled the night blanket up and hung it over herself, her brother, and the entire world. Then she curled up and fell asleep.

Dawi was startled awake when the sun was no longer shining on him. He saw the night blanket and was furious. He shook Nawi awake.

"You know I can't sleep in the darkness. It makes me nervous! I need some light."

But Nawi said, "I only put up my night blanket when I want to go to sleep. It is still light when I am awake. You know I can't sleep in the light. I need some darkness."

But that wasn't good enough for

Dawi. They argued and argued but could not agree.

Dawi decided to try something else. The next time Nawi put up her night blanket, he waited until she had fallen asleep. Then he crept to her sewing basket and took out a giant pin.

"This will give me some light!" he said,

and he began to poke holes in Nawi's black cloth. Each time he poked a hole in it, a tiny pinhole of light shone through.

Soon there were pinholes all over the night blanket.

But Dawi was still not happy.

Chapter Three
A Patch

"**I** need more light than this!" he said.

He took Nawi's giant scissors and cut a circle out of the night blanket. "That's better!" he said. Soon he fell asleep.

Not long afterward, Nawi awoke. She was furious when she saw what Dawi

had done. She couldn't do anything to repair all the pin holes—there were too many. But she took her needle and thread and began to slowly stitch a patch to close the large hole Dawi had made. The hole grew smaller and smaller until it was completely gone.

"Ah!" said Nawi. "Darkness again." And she fell fast asleep.

But then Dawi awoke.

"Where did the hole go that let in the light?" he said. "Nawi must have done this. But I can soon fix it!"

He took Nawi's scissors and began to unravel the patch Nawi had made over the hole. Slowly the hole got bigger and bigger and bigger, until it was a full circle again.

"That is much better!" said Dawi, and he curled up to go to sleep again.

And so the two have gone on cutting
and stitching to this very day. The
pinholes that Dawi made have become
our stars. They shine because they let in
the light from the world beyond Nawi's
night blanket.

The hole that Dawi cut in the night
blanket is the moon. When the moon is
getting smaller, it is because Nawi, the

night twin, is patching the hole to shut out the light. And when the moon is getting bigger, it is because Dawi, the day twin, is unraveling Nawi's patch.

Of course, he does not always get all Nawi's threads. That's why, when you look at the moon, you will see some gray threads from Nawi's patch that Dawi has missed.